For This Reason

God's Word and Your Marriage

Devotions for Couples
Preparing for Marriage and
the Already Married
Offering God's Encouragement
for Your Life Together

Rev. Gary W. Fehring

CSS Publishing Company, Inc.
Lima, Ohio

FOR THIS REASON

FIRST EDITION
Copyright © 2013
by CSS Publishing Co., Inc.

Published by CSS Publishing Company, Inc., Lima, Ohio 45807. All rights reserved. No part of this publication may be reproduced in any manner whatsoever without the prior permission of the publisher, except in the case of brief quotations embodied in critical articles and reviews. Inquiries should be addressed to: CSS Publishing Company, Inc., Permissions Department, 5450 N. Dixie Highway, Lima, Ohio 45807.

Scripture quotations are from the New Revised Standard Version of the Bible. Copyright 1989 by the Division of Christian Education of the National Council of the Churches of Christ in the USA, Nashville, Thomas Nelson Publishers © 1989. Used by permission. All rights reserved.

Library of Congress Cataloging-in-Publication Data

Fehring, Gary W.
   For this reason : God's word and your marriage devotions for couples preparing for marriage and the already married offering god's encouragement for your life together / Rev. Gary W. Fehring. -- 1st ed.
      pages cm
   ISBN 0-7880-2700-X (alk. paper)
  1. Married people--Prayers and devotions. I. Title.

BV4596.M3F44 2013
242'.644--dc23
                              2013011786

For more information about CSS Publishing Company resources, visit our website at www.csspub.com, email us at csr@csspub.com, or call (800) 241-4056.

ISBN-13: 978-0-7880-2700-0
ISBN-10: 0-7880-2700-X   PRINTED IN USA

These devotions are dedicated to my wife Mary, for encouraging me throughout their preparation, for her love of God's Word, and for continuing, along with God's Word, to teach me the very best of how good married life can be.

Table of Contents

Introduction	7
For This Reason *Genesis 2*	9
Being Content with What You Have *Hebrews 13:4-6*	13
Asking the Right Questions *Luke 10*	17
Worries Come *Luke 12*	23
The Need to Know *Ruth 1:16-17*	29
Overcoming Imperfection *Mark 14:26-30; 2 Corinthians 4:7*	35
Real Lessons for Real Life *Philippians 4; Romans 12*	39
Covered with Mud *1 Corinthians 13:4-6*	43
Forgiveness *Matthew 18:21-22*	47

Introduction

A Word to Couples Preparing for Marriage

Please be together when you use these devotions. The messages, prayers, and things to consider lose much of their value unless both of you are united in applying them to your life together.

These devotions are not about giving couples advice from the Bible. These devotions are about offering couples God's encouragement from the Bible. Each devotion began as a sermon I preached at a wedding I performed. In today's world marriage needs all the encouragement it can get. That is what I have attempted to do in my wedding sermons and in these devotions.

The devotions are meant to be used with a period of time passing between one devotion to the next. Should you be using the devotions on your own, the time between might depend upon your own schedules. You could include a few in an evening or afternoon you spend together. Be generous in the time you allow between them. Should you be using these devotions in the context of a marriage preparation program, a schedule for using them may be assigned.

Each of these devotions includes a biblical passage, a message to you arising from the biblical material, a prayer for you to pray together, and some things for you to consider as you relate the theme of that devotion to your life together.

Our God intends that your life together in marriage bring both of you all the goodness God created marriage to have. Helping to make that happen is the purpose of these devotions. May they prove to be a blessing to you as you prepare for marriage and, even more, throughout your married life.

A Word to Pastors Preparing Couples for Marriage

You may want to use some or all of these devotions as one of your tools in preparing couples for marriage. Which of them you use and how you want to use them is up to you. If you use a devotion with a couple, one suggestion might be to include the accompanying Thoughts for Discussion in your sessions with them.

*God's Word and
Your Companionship with Each Other
in Your Marriage*

For This Reason

> *Then the Lord God formed man from the dust of the ground, and breathed into his nostrils the breath of life; and the man became a living being. And the Lord God planted a garden in Eden, in the east; and there he put the man whom he had formed.... Then the Lord God said, "It is not good that the man should be alone; I will make him a helper as his partner." So out of the ground the Lord formed every animal of the field and every bird of the air, and brought them to the man to see what he would call them; and whatever the man called every living creature, that was its name. The man gave names to all cattle, and to the birds of the air, and to every animal in the field; but for the man there was not found a helper as his partner. So the Lord God caused a deep sleep to fall upon the man, and he slept; then he took one of his ribs and closed up its place with flesh. And the rib the Lord God had taken from the man he made into a woman and brought her to the man. Then the man said, "This at last is bone of my bones and flesh of my flesh; this one shall be called Woman, for out of Man this one was taken." Therefore a man leaves his father and his mother and clings to his wife, and they become one flesh.*
>
> (Genesis 2:7-8, 18-24)

The story of Adam and Eve in Genesis chapter 2 is full of wonderful connections. There is our connection with God, whose very hands have shaped us. There is our connection with the earth, out of whose rich soil we have been formed. There is our connection with the environment, the goodness of the garden, and our human task to till and keep that goodness. There is our connection with living things, all of which were created to be our companions.

All of those connections remain meaningful to us, in spite of how damaged they are by things that have gone wrong in us and wrong in the world itself. Yet even with those connections, we experience the same loneliness Adam felt. The Genesis story speaks of God's response to the loneliness he knows is there within us, and we know is there within ourselves.

In the rib account there is the truth of that strange mixture of dreaming and waking that is a part of every marriage. We see it in Adam at daybreak. Adam wakes up with a pain in his chest and Eve looking down at him. It is a kind of, "Hey, wait a minute. What is going on here?" experience that happens when a certain man meets a certain woman and unexpected things begin to happen in the deepest places of their hearts. For Adam, and for all the Adams and Eves to come, it is the great surprise, which is also the wonderful surprise because, as the Genesis story intends, it leads life into a whole new joy and a whole new goodness.

Genesis 2 ends with the truth of what God created marriage to be. Marriage is God's answer to human loneliness. Within the dreamlike poetry of the whole Eden story, with its recognition that "it is not good [to] be alone" (Genesis 2:18), is God's reminder to us of what marriage is all about. Marriage is about two people brought together by God so that neither one of them will ever be alone. It was for this reason God brought Adam and Eve together. It was for this reason God brought the two of you together.

There was the last time in his life when Jesus was alone. That time was the three hours Jesus was on the cross. He was alone because of sin, our sin. Sin did that to him. Sin does that to us. Much of the time in your marriage the two of you will be apart but try not to allow any time in your marriage when sin causes either of you to be alone. Except for those three hours on the cross, Jesus knew that no matter where he was or what he was doing, his heavenly Father was always there with him and for him. Because of what Jesus did for us on the cross, we know that no matter where we are or what we are doing, God is always there with us and for us.

What you know about God, know about each other. Your marriage is about you always being together, with each other and for each other, even when the two of you are apart. Remember, even when you are by yourselves, God is with you, and, in the deepest places of your hearts, you are with each other.

Let the Genesis story remind you of the God-given importance of your companionship in your marriage. Here is an Adam and Eve prayer of gratitude to God for that companionship. Give prayers like this a special place in your marriage and in your hearts.

Thank you, Lord.
Thank you for all the connections you have made
between us and yourself and your creation.
We treasure each of them.
You have made sure that neither one of us
will ever be alone.
Recognizing our loneliness,
you have given us to each other
as wonderful companions
for the rest of our lives.
Amen.

Thoughts for Discussion

1. Do you remember the moment you first realized you were meant for each other?
- Did you consider it a "God moment"?
- Looking back, do you feel God was bringing you together?

2. Your faith in Jesus assures you that God is always with you and for you.
- As you prepare for your life together in marriage, does the faith you each have in your partner assure you that they will always be there with you and for you?
- How important is it to each of you that your loved one has that faith in you?
- Being worthy of the faith your partner has placed in you is an important factor in how you will go about living your life in the years to come. What could you be doing that might damage their faith that you are always with them and for them?
- What will you do to encourage that faith?

3. It was to provide companionship that God brought Adam and Eve together.
- Situations occur in marriage through career, children, and individual interests that might cause injury to the companionship God intends for marriage.
- As you look toward your marriage, what are some things you might do to keep companionship a priority in your life together?
- How would you respond should either of you sense other things are coming between you?

(Following your discussion return to the prayer in this devotion, and once more pray it together.)

*God's Word and
Being Satisfied in Your Marriage*

Being Content with What You Have

> *Let marriage be held in honor by all, and let the marriage bed be undefiled; for God will judge fornicators and adulterers. Keep your lives free from the love of money, and be content with what you have; for he has said, "I will never leave you or forsake you." So we can say with confidence, "The Lord is my helper; I will not be afraid. What can anyone do to me?"*
> (Hebrews 13:4-6)

What does it take for people to be satisfied? Sometimes it takes more than we can possibly have. Sometimes we are haunted by the feeling of being unsatisfied. Like Eve in the Garden of Eden, we ache for the one thing more, that one thing that will finally make us feel satisfied.

It never does, of course. That little voice whispers to us and tells us that this one more thing, when we have it, will make us feel satisfied, and that little voice lies to us, just as it lied to Eve.

What does it take for people to be satisfied? On your wedding day, it will not be the beauty of your clothes that brings the feeling of satisfaction. It will not be the expense of the rings or the cost of the reception. What satisfies you on your wedding day is the simple love you have for each other, the love shown to you by your family and your friends, and the love of God that surrounds the day from beginning to end. What satisfies your guests isn't the pastor's sermon or the dinner menu. What satisfies your guests is seeing the two of you very much in love and sharing those special moments with you.

What does it take for people to be satisfied? The love of your life companion satisfies you. It doesn't have to be perfect love: always knowing, always saying, always doing the right thing, love that always gives you everything you want. It isn't perfect love that satisfies you in your marriage. It is a real person's real love that satisfies. It is a person being loved by another person that satisfies. That love is never perfect, because people are not perfect. Imperfect as it is, that love satisfies you, because it comes to you from the person you love.

What does it take for people to be satisfied? The love of God satisfies you. In our Lord Jesus, God has given us his goodness and his love. That goodness and that love satisfies you. More than anything you could want, God's love satisfies you. It satisfies you because it is always there and always will be there. God's love will always be there with exactly what you need.

What does it take for people to be satisfied? The goodness you bring to each other in your marriage satisfies you. It isn't that everything is always good. That would be nice, but it doesn't happen. Like love, it doesn't take perfect goodness to satisfy you. It takes a person who wants to bring you goodness, and who does bring goodness that for you is enough, sometimes just enough, sometimes more than enough. Real people bringing real goodness to each other's lives is what you do in your marriage. You don't need more than that to be satisfied.

What does it take for the two of you to be satisfied in your marriage? It takes what you already have: God's love and God's goodness, your love for each other, and the goodness you bring to each other. Whatever else you want beyond those things, whatever else you have beyond those things, it will always be from those things that you will be satisfied.

Being reminded by the author of the letter to the Hebrews to be content with what you have in your marriage, make the words of the text your prayer.

Lord,
you are our helper;
we will never be afraid.
With the love and goodness we receive from you,
and with the love and goodness
we are giving to each other,
we have everything we need
to be satisfied.
Amen.

Thoughts for Discussion

1. Do each of you feel content in your relationship with God?
- What is God doing to provide that feeling of contentment?
- Should you feel discontentment in your relationship with God, what could be done to change that feeling?

2. Do each of you feel satisfied in the relationship you now have with one another?
- Since no one is perfect, are you content to live with your partner despite their imperfections?
- Is there anything about your partner you would like to see changed to make you feel more satisfied in your relationship?

3. Is maintaining mutual contentment in the course taken by your life together in marriage a priority for you both?
- Looking ahead, how might you continue to "touch base" to ensure that mutual contentment with your relationship continues to exist? How important will it be for the two of you to do that?

4. The commandment not to covet means we each have enough for ourselves from what God, in God's goodness, provides.
- Is there anything either of you have set your hearts on that makes you feel unsatisfied or discontented unless you achieve it?
- If so, how might that affect your marriage?

(Following your discussion return to the prayer in this devotion, and once more pray it together.)

God's Word and
Being a Neighbor in Your Marriage

Asking the Right Questions

> *A man was going down from Jerusalem to Jericho, and fell into the hands of robbers, who stripped him and beat him, and went away, leaving him half dead. Now by chance a priest was going down that road; and when he saw him, he passed by on the other side. So likewise a Levite, when he came to the place and saw him, passed by on the other side. But a Samaritan, while traveling came near him; and when he saw him, he was moved with pity. He went to him and bandaged his wounds, having poured oil and wine on them. Then he put him on his own animal, brought him to an inn, and took care of him. The next day he took out two denarii, gave them to the innkeeper, and said, "Take care of him; and when I come back, I will repay you whatever more you spend." [Jesus asked] "Which of these three, do you think, was a neighbor to the man who fell into the hands of robbers?" [The lawyer] said, "The one who showed him mercy." Jesus said to him, "Go and do likewise."*
>
> (Luke 10:30-37)

"Who is my neighbor?" (Luke 10:29). That is what the lawyer asked Jesus. God's law required him to love his neighbor with the same love he had for himself. His response to that was to ask the Lord this question: "Who is my neighbor?"

That is a very human question. We have probably all asked it. "Who is neighbor to **me**?" "Who is interested in **me**?" "Who is willing to help **me** when **I** need someone's help?" "Who is willing to be **my** friend, stand up for **me**, take

my side?" Show me that person and I will love them with the same love I have for myself. Of course we would. Loving a person like that would be the same as loving ourselves.

"Who is my neighbor?" the lawyer asked Jesus. Jesus answered him with a story. The thing about the story Jesus told is that it didn't answer the lawyer's question. It didn't tell him who his neighbor was. Jesus' story told the lawyer to go out and **be** a neighbor, a caring, helping, supporting person to others.

Where love is concerned, the question is never "Who is my neighbor? Who is going to love me?" The question asked by someone who loves is always, "How can I be a neighbor to this other person? What is required of me to give this person the love they need?" Our Lord's answer to that question was that to give us the love we need he was required to give up his life on the cross. Jesus was a neighbor to you and to a world of people. Jesus' love required him to meet our need for forgiveness and salvation by giving his life for us.

The Samaritan in Jesus' story didn't ask the injured man "Are you going to be my neighbor?" The Samaritan simply was a neighbor, a good neighbor, to the injured man. Good things happen in the world when people do good for each other. Good things happen in marriages when husbands and wives do good for each other.

Bad things happen in marriages when couples ask each other: "Are you going to be a husband, a wife, to **me**?" "Are you going to give **me** all the love **I** need?" "Are you going to give **me** all the help, all the happiness, all the support and encouragement **I** need?" When we expect our partners to measure up to our expectations of the kind of wife or husband they should be, we do serious damage to our marriages. "If they are not going to be a good wife, a good husband, to me, why should I bother trying to be a good husband, a good wife, to them?" Love and companionship is replaced by hostility and isolation. That is not the kind of marriage anyone wants to have. It is all because we ask the wrong questions.

The right questions to ask in marriage are: "Am I being a wife, am I being a husband, to my partner?" "Am I giving **them** all my love?" "Am I giving **them** all my help, all my support, all my encouragement, all my trust and faithfulness?" "Am I doing everything I can to bring **them** the happiness they need?" Marriage is at its best when **both** partners devote themselves to being the best husband, the best wife, they can be for each other.

We don't know whether the Samaritan in Jesus' story was married, or if he was, the kind of husband he might have been. He probably would have been a very good husband, going out of his way to look after the needs of his wife. That is what he did for the injured man. He went out of his way, did far more than was expected, to look after the man's needs. Good neighbors don't have limits to what they are willing to do for others. Maybe they can't do everything, but they will do everything they can. That's the kind of neighbors all of us would like to have. That is the kind of neighbors the world needs all of us to be.

Good husbands and good wives don't have limits on what they are willing to do for each other. There may be times when they can't do everything, but at all times they are willing to do everything they can. That is the kind of partner all of us would like to have in our marriages. That is the kind of partner each of us ought to be in our marriages.

Our Lord gave his story of the Good Samaritan a happy ending. Loving help was given by a man who asked himself the right question: "How can I be the neighbor this person needs me to be?" There is a lifetime of happiness for you in your marriage when you both ask yourselves the right questions and express your love by being the neighbor, the husband, the wife, your partner needs you to be.

When the Samaritan came upon the injured man he might well have prayed a prayer much like this prayer for partners in marriage.

*Hear our prayer, O Lord,
and show us what is required of us
to be everything our loved ones
need us to be,
in everything that is happening today,
and in everything
that might be happening
tomorrow.
We ask in the name of Jesus,
who gave everything required of him
to meet our deepest needs.
Amen.*

Thoughts for Discussion

1. How would each of you answer the question asked of our Lord: "Who is my neighbor?"

2. In your marriage are each of you confident that your spouse will always be for you what the Samaritan was for the injured man?

3. In your marriage will you always be willing to be for your spouse what the Samaritan was for the injured man?

4. There was no limit to what the Samaritan was willing to do to be the neighbor the injured man needed him to be. Should there be any limit to what partners in a marriage do in being the good husband, good wife, their spouse needs them to be?

5. In your relationship have either of you had the experience of the injured man in the parable? You were in need and instead of helping, you felt your partner was passing you by?
   - If that has happened, how did you respond?
   - How should you respond if that happens in your marriage?
   - How should you respond if it was brought to your attention that your spouse was in need and they felt you were passing them by?

6. Which of the following describes how you want your relationship to be in your marriage?
a. Your spouse being a good neighbor for you.
b. You being a good neighbor for your spouse.
c. You and your spouse being good neighbors for each other.

(Following your discussion return to the prayer in this devotion, and once more pray it together.)

*God's Word and
Worries that Come in Marriage*

Worries Come

[Jesus said] "Do not worry about how you are to defend yourselves or what you are to say"; He said to his disciples, "Therefore I tell you, do not worry about your life, what will you eat or about your body, what you will wear. For life is more than food, and the body more than clothing. Consider the ravens: they neither sow nor reap, they have neither storehouse nor barn, and yet God feeds them. Of how much more value are you than the birds! And can any of you by worrying add a single hour to your span of life? If then you are not able to do as small a thing as that, why do you worry about the rest? Consider the lilies, how they grow: they neither toil nor spin; yet I tell you, even Solomon in all his glory was not clothed like one of these. But if God so clothes the grass of the field, which is alive today and tomorrow is thrown into the oven, how much more will he clothe you — you of little faith! And do not keep striving for what you are to eat and what you are to drink, and do not keep worrying. For it is the nations of the world that strive after these things, and your Father knows that you need them. Instead, strive for his kingdom, and these things will be given to you as well. Do not be afraid, little flock, for it is your Father's good pleasure to give you the kingdom. Sell your possessions, and give alms. Make purses for yourselves that do not wear out, an unfailing treasure in heaven, where no thief comes near and no moth destroys. For where your treasure is, there your heart will be also."

(Luke 12:22-34)

"Do not worry." Jesus repeats that over and over again to his disciples. Do not worry about your grocery bill. Don't worry about the tear in your new skirt or the stain on your new shirt. Don't worry about the funny noise coming from the engine of your car or the outstanding balance on your credit cards. Don't worry about anything. "Do not keep worrying" (Luke 12:29), Jesus said to his disciples in Galilee. Jesus says it as well to husbands and wives in their marriages: "Do not keep worrying."

Jesus is the Son of God. That has always given him an advantage over your average husband in knowing what to say and when to say it. Jesus didn't have a bank account. That was Judas' responsibility as the treasurer of the disciples. Jesus didn't worry about money. It was Judas who had to pay the bills. Judas probably worried.

While we may not have a care in the world on the day of our wedding, the married life that follows brings with it a long list of matters that can cause concern. If we didn't have any worries, we would wonder what on earth Jesus is talking about when he says, "Don't worry." It is precisely because worries are very real, in life and in marriage, that Jesus' words connect with us.

Now, if it was just some busybody, some know-it-all, who told us not to worry we might respond with "Oh yeah? Go mind your own business." When Jesus says "Don't worry," it is very different. When the crowds were worried about what they were going to have for supper, Jesus worked a miracle and fed 5,000 families with a bag lunch of bread and fish. When the leper worried about what was going to fall off next, his nose or his ears, Jesus issued a brief command and all traces of disease and decay were gone. When the father worried that his daughter was dying, Jesus took her hand. The little girl got up, rubbed her eyes, and wondered what was in the kitchen for breakfast.

The point is, Jesus can do something about those things that worry us. When he says "Don't worry," he touches our lives exactly where the worries are. If we let him, he will take those worries away. Through the Holy Spirit, Jesus is able to inspire in us such trust and confidence in God that even the most desperate of our worries weaken and wither away.

If we always remembered that, life would be much easier for us. The problem is that we don't always remember it. We put Jesus in one place in our lives, and we put our worries in another place. So we believe and worry at the same time.

When Jesus says "Don't worry," he reminds us of who he is, and what he is able to do. He also reminds us that we are in his care, protected by his arsenal of promises. Because of those reminders the moment happens when we turn our worries over to him. In those moments, when Jesus gets in to where our worries are, it is like a window opening in our souls. The refreshing wind of the Holy Spirit blows into us and, for that moment, our worries are over. We need moments like that in our lives. We need moments like that in our marriages. Husbands need moments like that. Wives need moments like that. We all need moments when Jesus opens a window in our souls and the Holy Spirit blows the worries away. We need those moments, and Jesus has an endless supply of them.

Those moments happen when we listen to Jesus. Of course we need to listen to Jesus all the time, but we need to listen to him so much more deeply when our worries weigh us down.

Hopefully this is not a day of worrying for you. Hopefully this is a day of loving, caring, smiling, laughing, and treasuring each precious moment as a gift of God. But as you know too well, days of worry are going to be there in your lives. Days of worry are going to be there in your marriage. Days of worry will be there, and Jesus will be there too. Stay close to Jesus in your married life. Listen to Jesus when he says, "Don't worry, I am here for you. There is nothing for the two of you to worry about."

To paraphrase that song from the 1960s, it takes a worried couple to pray a worried prayer. If you're not worried now, you will be worried soon. This is a "not worried" prayer for the help you know you are going to need when the worries come.

*Lord Jesus,
as you have been there for so many others
when their days of worries came,
so be there for us.
Keep the door always open
between yourself and our worries
so that you will be
where we need you to be.
Bless us with your moments of relief
as the worries lift,
and we rest our lives and our marriage
securely
in your care.
Amen.*

Thoughts for Discussion

1. The things that cause us to worry and the way we handle those worries can either drive us apart from those we love or bring us closer to them.
- There is a special closeness in marriage when couples share what worries them with each other, and together they bring those worries to the Lord in prayer.
- In marriage, when worries are not shared but kept inside, hidden from our partners, a distance is created that is often a cause for unhappiness by those who feel "shut out."

2. In each of your pasts, how have worries been handled?
a. in your families:
- Have family members been willing to share their worries? (Yes? No?)
- Can you recall times when you felt closer to a family member because they shared with you something that worried them?
- Can you recall times when you had the feeling something was worrying someone in your family and you felt shut out because they refused to share what it was?
- In your family is there a common faith that God is with us and for us as we face those things that worry us?
- Do your families have the practice of praying together? If so, is the sharing of worries included in those prayers? If not, is that something you wish your families would do?

b. in yourselves:
- Have each of you been willing to share your worries with other family members? If so, has it made you feel closer to them? If not, why not? Have you kept your worries

hidden from others because acknowledging you have worries would be a sign of weakness? A lack of faith? A lack of trust in others?
- Do you pray when you experience worry? Do you have faith that God is with you and for you to help you deal with what worries you?

c. in your relationship:
- Do each of you feel that your partner has been willing to share whatever worries they have with you?
- Have either of you ever experienced being shut out from something you felt was worrying your partner?
- Do you share a common faith that God will always be with you and for you to help you deal with what worries you?
- Are there any issues about sharing worries that need to be worked out as you plan your marriage?

d. in your marriage:
- Is the willingness to share your worries with one another going to be important in your life together?
- Is coming together in faith and sharing your worries with God in prayer something you want to include in your life together in marriage?

(Following your discussion return to the prayer in this devotion, and once more pray it together.)

*God's Word and
Your Lifelong Journey in Marriage*

The Need to Know

> *But Ruth said [to her mother-in-law, Naomi], "Do not press me to leave you or to turn back from following you! Where you go, I will go; where you lodge, I will lodge; your people shall be my people, and your God my God! Where you die, I will die — there will I be buried. May the Lord do thus and so to me, and more as well, if even death parts me from you!"*
> (Ruth 1:16-17)

Questions are not uncommon in marriage: "Is it okay if I go fishing with the guys next weekend?" "What did you buy on Ebay for $350?" "Why don't we go out like we used to?" "Where are the keys to the car?" "Do you know what **your** son just did?" and the mother of all questions asked in marriage, "Do you still love me?"

Marriages can be filled with questions, but most of them are not the kind of questions called for by God's word: "Where you go, I will go" (Ruth 1:16). "Love does not insist on its own way" (1 Corinthians 13:4). "Ask and it will be given you" (Matthew 7:7).

In marriage, scripture encourages husbands and wives to attempt, in the deepest possible way, to discover where their partner in life is going, so that they can go along beside them as their loving companion. Love that does not insist on its own way must discover the way the other person is going. Love can then express itself in support and encouragement, and caring, patient partnership.

Like Ruth and her mother-in-law Naomi, husbands and wives accompany each other along life's journey. This journey is not measured in miles but in years and in experiences. In the years to come there may be many journeys the two of you will be taking as you move, house to house, neighborhood to neighborhood, city to city, possibly state to state, or country to country. No matter many how many miles these moves might involve, they will be the shortest journeys you will be taking in your marriage.

The great marriage journeys are those measured in years, years of moving together through the experiences of life. On your lifelong journey together may God bless you with miles of happiness, and no more than a few yards now and then of tears and sorrow.

This marriage journey will be traveled together. The way you stay side by side in that journey is by asking and seeking to know the answers to these questions: "Where is the heart of my beloved taking them?" "Where is the faith of my beloved taking them?" "Where is the soul of my beloved taking them?"

You will not always be asking those questions with your voices. You will sometimes ask them with your eyes, as you look into the eyes of your beloved. They will sometimes be asked by your hands, as you caress your beloved's face. "Where is your heart taking you?" "Where is your faith sending you?" "Where is your soul moving you?" "I need to know these things, my love, so that I can travel with you to those places."

Ask. Seek. Be led by each other. Be led by God. Let your marriage be a lifelong journey of love, the love that finds its direction not in going its own way, but by accompanying the journey of its beloved.

Before their journey began, Ruth might have prayed for God to guide her and to lead both her and Naomi in the journey they would be taking together. This could have been Ruth's prayer. Make it your prayer.

Lord of all life,
and all life's journeys,
keep us safe on the journey
we are taking together.
Help each of us to know
where you are taking
our beloved,
so that we can travel there
with them
and with you.
Amen.

Thoughts for Discussion

1. Ruth's decision to go with Naomi concerned a physical location. How was the decision made about where, as a married couple, you will be living?
- How would either of you react if your partner wanted or needed to move to a location far from your family home? Could this ever become an issue in your marriage?

2. Do either of you have plans for the future that will require your spouse to make sacrifices? If so, is it a sacrifice happily made?
- Knowing as much as you do about one another, are you confident that whomever might have to make a sacrifice will not hold that against the other?

3. Have you shared your thoughts about where each of you would like your married lives to go (i.e.: children, careers, interests, hopes, and dreams)?
- Is there anything you can see becoming so important to one of you that it could lead you to go your separate ways?
- Should situations in life arise that seem to be taking you apart, would you both be willing to compromise to stay together? If a compromise cannot be achieved, would both of you be willing to maintain your relationship by giving up what you want for the sake of what your partner wants?

4. When in some marriages what one partner is doing (battering, for instance) or wants to do is simply wrong, does God require the spouse to give in to that want to save the marriage? What kind of sacrifices should not be made to save a marriage?

5. The decision Ruth made to go with Naomi led to wonderful things happening in her life. Can you both see how the decisions you have made and will make about the course of your life together will lead to wonderful things for both of you?

(Following your discussion return to the prayer in this devotion, and once more pray it together.)

*God's Word and
Making a Good Marriage*

Overcoming Imperfection

> *When they had sung the hymn, they went out to the Mount of Olives. And Jesus said to them, "You will all become deserters; for it is written, 'I will strike the shepherd, and the sheep will be scattered.' But after I am raised up, I will go before you to Galilee." Peter said to him, "Even though all become deserters, I will not." Jesus said to him, "Truly I tell you, this day, this very night, before the cock crows twice, you will deny me three times."*
> (Mark 14:26-30)

> *But we have this treasure in clay jars.*
> (2 Corinthians 4:7)

The Apostle Peter was not perfect. The Apostle Paul, in referring to himself, wrote that he was far from being a perfect container for the great treasure God has given to the world in Jesus Christ; instead he described himself as only a "clay jar."

Imperfect people, yet what good lives these two men lived and what good things these two men did.

I don't suppose I have to tell you that neither of you is a perfect person. If you don't know that about yourselves, you have some serious self-examination to accomplish before you continue planning your marriage.

None of us is a perfect person. That means our marriages aren't going to be perfect either. It is a law of nature that imperfect people are going to have imperfect marriages. When you have been married for more than a few days, it will be clear to you that I am not telling you anything you won't already know from experience. Your marriage is not going to be a perfect marriage. That's the way it will always be.

The bad news is that you can't have a perfect marriage. The good news is that you can have a very good marriage. You can have a marriage where you continue to discover good things about each other. You can have a marriage where you continue to do good things for each other.

Our Garden of Eden living is over. All that remains is the memory and some bits and pieces of goodness we haven't damaged beyond repair. Those wonderful bits and pieces of goodness that remain in human living, remain too in marriage. They are what gives marriage its joy, comfort, pleasure, and delight. There will be goodness in your marriage as you enjoy together the beauty of God's creation. There will be goodness in your marriage as you enjoy one another as the precious persons God made each of you. There will be goodness in your marriage as you enjoy the family with which God will surround you. You may not be able to have a perfect marriage, but you can have a marriage filled with goodness.

One of the ways you can help make that happen is by following the advice of our Lord in Matthew 5. In his Sermon on the Mount, Jesus tells us to go the extra mile. That is advice for a good marriage. In good marriages both partners are willing and eager to do not just enough, but more than enough to meet each other's needs and to make each other happy.

Jesus also tells us not to hit back. That too is advice for a good marriage. In a good marriage husbands and wives know that hurt is going to happen. Part of being imperfect means that we say and do things that hurt each other. In some marriages this results in a contest, each partner trying to get in the last punch. In good marriages husbands and wives respond to hurts with help and healing.

Jesus tells us to love our enemies. Strange as it sounds to use the word "enemy" in the context of marriage, what Jesus says is good advice for a good marriage. There are times in marriage when we get so confused and mixed up that instead of seeing our partners as the best and closest friends we have, we see them as enemies, someone to defend against, someone to attack. In those times husbands and wives must put God's love to work in their love for each other. That is the way two people who are not really enemies continue their marriage as lifelong friends.

Don't ever think about giving up on your marriage because it isn't perfect. Remember that God never gives up on us because we are not perfect. Jesus wants us all to be good people. Jesus wants the two of you to have a good marriage. Jesus wants you to know that you have the ability to do that. He would never give you his advice for living if he knew you couldn't follow it. You can bring goodness to each other in your words and deeds. Because you are not perfect, ask your heavenly Father to help you do it.

*Father in heaven,
when we look for perfection
we look to you
and to your Son.
Keep us from expecting perfection
in our marriage.
Make us determined
to never allow our imperfections
to prevent us
from enjoying your goodness
and working with you
in making goodness happen
in our life together.
Amen.*

Thoughts for Discussion

1. Take a moment for each of you to think over what it means that neither of you is a perfect person.
- Are you able to admit to yourself that you are not perfect and that you bring your imperfections with you into your marriage?
- Are you willing to accept that your partner is not perfect and will be bringing their imperfections with them into your marriage?

2. Consider how you each might react when you expect your partner to be perfect in something and, in your opinion, they are not. Should you: a) get angry, b) instruct them on how to be better, or c) understand, accept that nobody is perfect, and simply get on with your relationship?

3. Because none of us are perfect, people sometimes say or do things that hurt others. Take a moment to think over your personal histories. Has there ever been a time when someone (family member, friend) said or did something that hurt you?
- Did you respond with: a) understanding and accepting their imperfections and getting on with your relationship, b) forgiveness, c) anger, d) hurting them back, or e) talking over what happened and explaining how you felt hurt?

(Following your discussion return to the prayer in this devotion, and once more pray it together.)

Listening to God's Word
to Learn About (Married) Life

Real Lessons for Real Life

I rejoice in the Lord greatly that now at last you have revived your concern for me; indeed, you were concerned for me, but had no opportunity to show it. Not that I am referring to being in need; for I have learned to be content with whatever I have. I know what it is to have little, and I know what it is to have plenty. In any and all circumstances I have learned the secret of being well-fed and of going hungry, of having plenty and being in need. I can do all things through him who strengthens me.

(Philippians 4:10-13)

Let love be genuine; hate what is evil, hold fast to what is good; love one another with mutual affection; outdo one another in showing honor. Do not lag in zeal, be ardent in spirit, serve the Lord. Rejoice in hope, be patient in suffering, persevere in prayer. Contribute to the needs of the saints; extend hospitality to strangers. Bless those who persecute you; bless and do not curse them. Rejoice with those who rejoice, weep with those who weep. Live in harmony with one another; do not be haughty, but associate with the lowly; do not claim to be wiser than you are. Do not repay anyone evil for evil, but take thought for what is noble in the sight of all. If it is possible, so far as it depends on you, live peaceably with all.

(Romans 12:9-18)

Both Romans 12 and Philippians 4 blossom for us like a meadow in springtime, bursting with beautiful things that have to do with the very best of human living. There is love, real, genuine, honest love. Love in your lives and love in your marriage. Love that doesn't stop when the wedding is over and those who were there to witness your love have gone home.

There are choices, the kind of choices people make in life and in marriage. There is the necessity of every husband and wife to have a stubborn determination to make those choices well and to always choose what is best for their marriage and for their family.

There is companionship in the give and take that comes with life together in marriage to care, really care, about each other. To always be there for each other.

In the scripture lessons there is celebration, the celebration of a partner. It is the willingness of one person in the marriage to beat the drum for the other as that person marches for a while at the head of the parade. There are few better gifts each of you can give to the other than the knowledge that in you, their partner in marriage, they always have someone standing on the sidelines cheering them on.

There is excitement, the excitement that comes in service to our Lord. It is the feeling that comes to us when we are doing what God designed us to do: care, tend, and nurture his creation. We are to love each other, building upon the good that is so important to the world and so important to human living. Married life never gets dull when husbands and wives continue to explore new ways of serving their Lord.

Also in these verses of God's word there is patient suffering. Suffering is part of the life story of every one of us. While times of suffering are not to be welcomed in marriage, the reality of suffering, when it is experienced, must not be denied. When suffering happens, face that suffering together, accept God's offer of assistance, and with patience and love help each other through.

Prayer is found in our scripture lessons, a life of conversation with an attentive God, sharing all of living with him. Sometimes in marriage each of you will be doing that alone. The best times in marriage are when the two of you do that together.

Our lessons speak of charity and hospitality. Everything we call our own we have received from God as a gift. Be sure your home and your hearts have open doors so that others are invited in to share.

In our scripture lessons the Apostle Paul invites us to bless those who misuse us. The world calls that weakness. God's word understands that as being "Christlike." It is a difficult thing for people to do by themselves. In marriage and family, members give one another the support that makes following our Lord possible. Receiving encouragement from each other, partners in marriage and family can show the world a better way of bringing change; not with a fist, but with a blessing.

Learning in progress must be the maxim of everyone who opens a Bible. It is certainty the maxim of every couple united in marriage. There are always more things to be learned. There are always more prayers to be prayed. This is one of them.

*Gracious Lord,
you have consented to teach us
through your word
and through your word made flesh,
our Lord and Savior, Jesus Christ.
May our love for you
be demonstrated in our willingness
to open our lives and
our marriage
to every good and important thing
you have to teach us.
Amen.*

Thoughts for Discussion

In the scriptures that began this devotion, among all the lessons for living there are five for you to give special attention to as you plan your life together. They are:

1. Celebrating your partner — husbands and wives being complementary, not competitive, in their relationship.
2. Excitement in serving the Lord — husbands and wives sharing a common enthusiasm for putting their faith in action.
3. Patience in suffering — husbands and wives supporting each other when life hurts.
4. Charity and hospitality — husbands and wives sharing a willingness to be good neighbors to others.
5. Giving support when others need it — husbands and wives sharing a willingness to open their hearts to their companions in life.

As you look at each of the five, ask yourselves these questions:
1. Does this describe the kind of people we are?
2. Does this describe the kind of marriage we both want to have?
3. Is this something we need to talk about and work on for our marriage?

(Following your discussion return to the prayer in this devotion, and once more pray it together.)

*God's Word and
Allowing the Goodness to Show
in Your Marriage*

Covered with Mud

*Love is not envious or boastful or arrogant or rude.
It does not insist on its own way; it is not irritable or
resentful; it does not rejoice in wrongdoing.*
(1 Corinthians 13:4-6)

Here is the question: "What does riding through a muddy field in an off-road vehicle have to do with these verses from Paul's letter to the Corinthians, and what does it have to do with your marriage?"

I have never ridden through a muddy field in an off-road vehicle. I don't intend to ride in one of these vehicles because I have seen those vehicles when they come out of the mud, or rather, when they bring the mud out with them. It is only by faith that we know there is a person and a vehicle under that mound of mud.

So many times it is only by faith that we know God has given the gift of love to every human being. Too often God's gift of love is buried under what Paul in First Corinthians considers nothing more than the muddy clutter of other things. Jealousy, conceit, pride, ambition, intellectual and even spiritual arrogance, selfishness, self-centeredness, callousness and carelessness in our treatment of others, resentments; it's all mud. That's what Paul is telling us.

The love our God who created us has placed in every human soul can be so often buried under a mound of life's muddy clutter. The love is still there, because God's gift of love is eternal (1 Corinthians 13:13). We cannot remove God's gift of love from within us, but we can bury it so that no one, not even ourselves, know it is there, except by faith.

I have no idea how people clean the mud from their off-road vehicles. We do know how God cleans the muddy clutter of human living from the love he has placed within our souls. He does it by bringing us to Jesus. The love that is there in Jesus washes over us in a kind of baptism "hosing down."

In Christ, the love that our living has buried is revealed — resurrected in a way — to take its God-appointed place in the center of our daily lives, in the center of our marriages, in the center of our family and community living. This is love that is kind. Love that is gentle. Love that is patient. Love that is humble. Love that is filled with care and concern for others. Love with a warm, grateful attachment to God, opening up into a warm and grateful attachment to others and to life itself.

If you own a vehicle made for driving off the road there are days when you come home covered with mud. That is something you have to live with. What you don't have to live with are days when you come home to your marriage with your love for each other buried under the muddy clutter of life's other things. Should that ever happen, allow God's love in Jesus to wash over you, hose you down, hose down your marriage, so the love you know by faith that is within each of you can be seen and lived again.

Martin Luther understood that our baptism ought to be a part of our daily living. In prayer, invite the love of our Lord, in baptism's cleansing water, to be a daily part of your life together. Ask that each day your marriage may become new for you both, with your love for each other washed clean from the muddy clutter of life's other things.

*Spirit of God,
give us the faith we need
to always see
the love that you have placed there
in each of us.
Every day bring the love of Jesus
into our lives and into our marriage
so that our love,
and our love for each other,
never gets buried
under all of life's
other things.
Amen.*

Thoughts for Discussion

1. Because you are baptized, you each have God's gift of love within you.
- Describe how each of you have seen that love in the kind of person your partner has been for you.
- How important is it going to be to keep that love from getting buried under all the things that are part of married life?

2. Regular participation in worship is a way in which love is resurrected from beneath the clutter of life's other things.
- Is regular participation in worship going to be part of your married life?
- Do you see that as a way the love in your relationship is continually renewed?

3. Prayer is another way love can continue to maintain its special place in your marriage.
- How important is it for both of you to make a time of prayer a part of your daily lives? (Individually? Together?)
- How important is it for prayers for your marriage to be included in your prayer life?

(Following your discussion return to the prayer in this devotion, and once more pray it together.)

*God's Word and the
Importance of Forgiveness
in Your Marriage*

Forgiveness

> *Then Peter came to [Jesus] and said to him, "Lord, if another member of the church sins against me, how often should I forgive? As many as seven times?" Jesus said to him, "Not seven times, but, I tell you, seventy-seven times."*
>
> (Matthew 18:21-22)

How much forgiveness am I going to have to give? That is the question Peter asked Jesus. How much forgiveness am I going to have to give? Should I forgive just a little or as much as I can keep track of to keep balanced? Should I forgive just enough to show that I am a tolerant person, but not so much that I am taken advantage of? Peter was asking when he should make the switch from being Mother Teresa to being Rambo.

Forgiveness is an important subject to be raised in marriage. How much forgiveness is needed in life? How much forgiveness is needed in marriage? The answer, as Jesus tells Peter, and as every married couple knows, is that so much forgiveness is needed in life, and especially in marriage and family life, that it is impossible to keep track of it. Marriage, like every relationship in life, thrives on forgiveness.

In your marriage, the moment you look at each other and no longer see the forgiveness of Mother Teresa but see the vengeful face of Rambo, that's the time to get some help. Your marriage will be in serious danger. Help will be needed to fix it, or you will need lawyers to end it.

How much forgiveness does your marriage need? More forgiveness than you can ever keep track of. Your marriage needs so much forgiveness that if you try to keep score, as Peter did, it will only slow you down.

Does one of you have to give more forgiveness than they will receive? Is your marriage going to shortchange one of you in the exchange of forgiveness? You don't have to worry about that. The amount of forgiveness we are receiving from Jesus is so huge that the amount we give to others is insignificant in size. No matter how much forgiveness you give in your lives, and in your marriage, you will always be receiving more from your Lord and Savior.

Like all of life, marriage thrives on the forgiveness coming from Jesus Christ. That forgiveness is there for the two of you and for all of us for the continual renewal and re-creation of ourselves and our relationships. Whatever else you may make as a regular, daily, or weekly part of your marriage, begin by including opportunities for receiving, and being reminded of, the forgiveness Jesus is so generously giving you. Being together at worship will do that for you. Prayer will do that for you. Christ-centered reading and conversation will do that for you.

From the daily bread of forgiveness you have in Christ, you have enough food for a lifetime of feeding each other with forgiveness. Seven times before the alarm clock stops buzzing. Seventy times before the toast is done. Seventy times seven before the supper dishes are washed and put away. The daily exchange of forgiveness in marriage is constant and unending.

Forgiveness is there for the two of you to use for the goodness and the maintenance of your marriage. Be generous with giving it and receiving it. The love in your marriage depends on your generosity in giving and receiving forgiveness. The companionship that is yours as husband and wife is anchored in the forgiveness of Jesus as both of you put that forgiveness to use in your life together in marriage and your life together in Christ.

*Forgive us our sins, Lord,
as we forgive those who sin against us.
When either of us feel as though we have been
sinned against in our marriage,
make us as generous in forgiving our partner
as you are in forgiving us.
When we pass around the daily bread
your heavenly Father has given to feed
our lives,
keep us passing around the forgiveness
you have given us to feed
our life together.
Amen.*

Thoughts for Discussion

1. As you each think about your past, is there anyone you have not been able to forgive? Why not?
• Have you been able to continue in your relationship with that person despite holding onto what they said or did against you?

2. Each of you think to yourselves:
• In your life together has your partner ever wronged you in any way by something they said or did? Was it serious enough to harm your relationship? If it was, did you talk to them about it?
• If you did talk to them about it, did their response lead to your forgiveness?
• If you didn't talk to them about it, were you able to simply forgive them and go on with your relationship being as good as it was before? What made that possible?
• Without forgiving them, are you holding what they said or did against them? Is that something you see yourself continuing to do in your marriage?

3. In your life in Christ's church, how important is it for you to know that between you and God there is always love and forgiveness?

4. In your life in marriage, how important is it for you both to know that between you and your partner there is always love and forgiveness?

5. In praying the Lord's Prayer is your request for God's forgiveness matched by your personal willingness to forgive others? Does that mean without limit? Will that always include your partner in marriage?

6. Is it possible to have a good marriage when unforgiven wrongs continue in the relationship? In your marriage, what steps would you take should the wrong which is done be so serious that forgiveness cannot easily be found?

7. Are you both willing to pass around forgiveness as the daily bread God provides to feed the goodness of your life together in marriage and family?

(Following your discussion return to the prayer in this devotion, and once more pray it together.)

www.ingramcontent.com/pod-product-compliance
Lightning Source LLC
Chambersburg PA
CBHW071801040426
42446CB00012B/2656